The
Legal Foundations
of
Special Education

D0815756

A Practical Approach to Special Education for Every Teacher

The Fundamentals of Special Education
A Practical Guide for Every Teacher

The Legal Foundations of Special Education
A Practical Guide for Every Teacher

Effective Assessment for Students With Special Needs
A Practical Guide for Every Teacher

Effective Instruction for Students With Special Needs
A Practical Guide for Every Teacher

*Working With Families and Community Agencies to Support
Students With Special Needs*
A Practical Guide for Every Teacher

Public Policy, School Reform, and Special Education
A Practical Guide for Every Teacher

Teaching Students With Sensory Disabilities
A Practical Guide for Every Teacher

Teaching Students With Medical, Physical, and Multiple Disabilities
A Practical Guide for Every Teacher

Teaching Students With Learning Disabilities
A Practical Guide for Every Teacher

Teaching Students With Communication Disorders
A Practical Guide for Every Teacher

Teaching Students With Emotional Disturbance
A Practical Guide for Every Teacher

Teaching Students With Mental Retardation
A Practical Guide for Every Teacher

Teaching Students With Gifts and Talents
A Practical Guide for Every Teacher

The
Legal Foundations
of
Special Education

A Practical Guide for Every Teacher

JIM YSSELDYKE
BOB ALGOZZINE

CORWIN PRESS
A SAGE Publications Company
Thousand Oaks, California

For information:

Corwin Press
A Sage Publications Company
2455 Teller Road
Thousand Oaks, California 91320
www.corwinpress.com

Sage Publications Ltd.
1 Oliver's Yard
55 City Road
London EC1Y 1SP
United Kingdom

Sage Publications India Pvt. Ltd.
B-42, Panchsheel Enclave
Post Box 4109
New Delhi 110 017 India

Printed in the United States of America

Library of Congress Cataloging-in-Publication Data

Ysseldyke, James E.
The legal foundations of special education: A practical guide for every teacher/ James E. Ysseldyke & Bob Algozzine.
    p. cm.
Includes bibliographical references and index.
ISBN 1-4129-3942-9 (cloth)
ISBN 1-4129-3895-3 (pbk.)
    1. Special education—Law and legislation—United States.
I. Algozzine, Robert. II. Title.
KF4209.3.Y77 2006
344.73'0791—dc22

                                                    2005037818

This book is printed on acid-free paper.

06   07   08   09   10   9   8   7   6   5   4   3   2   1

Acquisitions Editor:	Kylee M. Liegl
Editorial Assistant:	Nadia Kashper
Production Editor:	Denise Santoyo
Copy Editor:	Colleen Brennan
Typesetter:	C&M Digitals (P) Ltd.
Indexer:	Kathy Paparchontis
Cover Designer:	Michael Dubowe

Contents

About
A Practical Approach to Special Education for Every Teacher

S pecial education means specially designed instruction for students with unique learning needs. Students receive special education for many reasons. Students with disabilities such as mental retardation, hearing impairments (including deafness), speech or language impairments, visual impairments (including blindness), emotional disturbance, orthopedic impairments, autism, traumatic brain injury, other health impairments, or specific learning disabilities are entitled to special education services. Students who are gifted and talented also receive special education. Special education services are delivered in many settings, including regular classes, resource rooms, and separate classes. The 13 books of this collection will help you teach students with disabilities and those with gifts and talents. Each book focuses on a specific area of special education and can be used individually or in conjunction with all or some of the other books. Six of the books provide the background and content knowledge you need in order to work effectively with all students with unique learning needs:

Book 1: The Fundamentals of Special Education

Book 2: The Legal Foundations of Special Education

Book 3: Effective Assessment for Students With Special Needs

Book 4: Effective Instruction for Students With Special Needs

Book 5: Working With Families and Community Agencies to Support Students With Special Needs

Book 6: Public Policy, School Reform, and Special Education

Seven of the books focus on teaching specific groups of students who receive special education:

Book 7:   Teaching Students With Sensory Disabilities

Book 8:   Teaching Students With Medical, Physical, and Multiple Disabilities

Book 9:   Teaching Students With Learning Disabilities

Book 10: Teaching Students With Communication Disorders

Book 11: Teaching Students With Emotional Disturbance

Book 12: Teaching Students With Mental Retardation

Book 13: Teaching Students With Gifts and Talents

All of the books in *A Practical Approach to Special Education for Every Teacher* will help you to make a difference in the lives of all students, especially those with unique learning needs.

ACKNOWLEDGMENTS

The approach we take in *A Practical Approach to Special Education for Every Teacher* is an effort to change how professionals learn about special education. The 13 separate books are a result of prodding from our students and from professionals in the field to provide a set of materials that "cut to the chase" in teaching them about students with disabilities and about building the capacity of systems to meet those students' needs. Teachers told us that in their classes they always confront students with special learning needs and students their school district has assigned a label to (e.g., students with learning disabilities). Our students and the professionals we worked with wanted a very practical set of texts that gave them the necessary **information** *about* **the students** (e.g., federal definitions, student characteristics) and specific **information on** *what to do about* **the students** (assessment and teaching strategies, approaches that work). They also wanted the opportunity to purchase parts of textbooks, rather than entire texts, to learn what they needed.

The production of this collection would not have been possible without the support and assistance of many colleagues. Professionals associated with Corwin Press—Faye Zucker, Kylee Liegl, Robb Clouse—helped us work through the idea of introducing special education differently, and their support in helping us do it is deeply appreciated.

Faye Ysseldyke and Kate Algozzine, our children, and our grandchildren also deserve recognition. They have made the problems associated with the project very easy to diminish, deal with, or dismiss. Every day in every way, they enrich our lives and make us better. We are grateful for them.

About the Authors

Jim Ysseldyke, PhD, is Birkmaier Professor in the Department of Educational Psychology, director of the School Psychology Program, and director of the Center for Reading Research at the University of Minnesota. Widely requested as a staff developer and conference speaker, he brings more than 30 years of research and teaching experience to educational professionals around the globe.

As the former director of the federally funded National Center on Educational Outcomes, Ysseldyke conducted research and provided technical support that helped to boost the academic performance of students with disabilities and improve school assessment techniques nationally. Today he continues to work to improve the education of students with disabilities.

The author of more than 300 publications on special education and school psychology, Ysseldyke is best known for his textbooks on assessment, effective instruction, issues in special education, and other cutting-edge areas of education and school psychology. With *A Practical Approach to Special Education for Every Teacher,* he seeks to equip educators with practical knowledge and methods that will help them to better engage students in exploring—and meeting—all their potentials.

Bob Algozzine, PhD, is professor in the Department of Educational Leadership at the University of North Carolina at Charlotte and project codirector of the U.S. Department of Education–supported Behavior and Reading Improvement Center. With 25 years of research experience and extensive first-hand knowledge of teaching students classified as seriously emotionally disturbed (and other equally useless terms), Algozzine is a uniquely qualified staff developer, conference speaker, and teacher of behavior management and effective teaching courses.

As an active partner and collaborator with professionals in the Charlotte-Mecklenburg schools in North Carolina and as an editor of several journals focused on special education, Algozzine keeps his finger on the pulse of current special education practice. He has written more than 250 manuscripts on special education topics, authoring many popular books and textbooks on how to manage emotional and social behavior problems. Through *A Practical Approach to Special Education for Every Teacher,* Algozzine hopes to continue to help improve the lives of students with special needs—and the professionals who teach them.

Self-Assessment 1

B efore you begin this book, check your knowledge and understanding of the content being covered. Choose the best answer for each of the following questions.

1. The fundamental principle that underlies court cases and legislation about the rights of students who are exceptional is the:

   a. Due process clause of Public Law 94–142

   b. Right to Education Act of 1975

   c. Equal Protection Clause of the Fourteenth Amendment to the U.S. Constitution

   d. Individuals With Disabilities Education Act

2. Schools were first required to provide a free, appropriate public education to preschoolers with disabilities in:

   a. 1975

   b. 1986

   c. 1994

   d. 2000

3. Which of the following laws prohibits discrimination on the basis of disability in employment, services rendered by state and local governments, transportation, and tele-communication services?

   a. Individuals With Disabilities Education Act (IDEA)

   b. No Child Left Behind Act (NCLB)

   c. Education for All Handicapped Children Act (PL 94–142)

   d. Americans With Disabilities Act (ADA)

4. Which of the following is true about architectural accessibility—the removal of steps and other barriers that limit the participation of people with disabilities?

   a. Every building must be barrier free.

   b. Every method of transportation must be accessible to those who are disabled.

   c. Students with disabilities must have equal access to programs and services.

   d. A and B above

5. Which of the following is *not* required in Public Law 94–142, the Education for All Handicapped Children Act?

   a. Annual reporting on the performance and progress of all students, including students with disabilities

   b. Due process

   c. Education in a least restrictive environment (LRE)

   d. Individualized education program (IEP)

6. By law, decisions about eligibility for special education services must be made by:

   a. Principals

   b. School psychologists

   c. Multidisciplinary teams

   d. Parents

7. Under the Reading First legislation of the Bush administration, specialized reading services must be provided to:

a. Students in Grades 1 through 3 in Title 1 schools

b. Students with severe disabilities

c. All students, including students with disabilities and students with limited English proficiency

d. Students with reading disabilities

8. The protection in evaluation procedures provision of the law specifies all of the following except:

a. Tests must be administered in the language and form most likely to yield accurate information on what a child knows and can do academically, developmentally, and functionally unless not feasible to provide and administer.

b. Students must be assessed in their native language or mode of communication.

c. Parents must give their consent before a student can be tested.

d. Tests must be valid for the purposes for which they are used.

9. Which of the following was not decided in a U.S. Supreme Court case?

a. Segregation of schools is illegal because it denies equal protection and equal opportunity.

b. Children are "persons" under the Constitution and have civil rights independent of their parents.

c. Disruptive students with disabilities do not actually have to cause harm before removal from school; rather, they have to be judged substantially likely to cause harm.

d. Reimbursement for private school tuition is an appropriate form of relief for a court to grant.

10. Students with disabilities must be educated in a least restrictive environment. This means:

    a. They may not be placed in institutions.

    b. They have a right to be educated in general education classes.

    c. They have a right to be educated in the least restrictive setting in which they can be successful.

    d. Parents of students with disabilities cannot home-school the students.

11. A famous California court case, *Larry P. v. Riles*, addressed which of the following educational issues?

    a. Assessment of English language learners in their native language

    b. Bias in assessment of black students who were being considered for classes for mentally retarded students

    c. Exclusion of students with disabilities from public education

    d. Medical services for students with disabilities

REFLECTION

After you have responded to the multiple-choice self-assessment, provide brief answers to the following questions:

- Why did courts and legislatures get involved in the first place in matters of providing services to students with disabilities?
- How do the provisions of federal law increase the work of educational professionals?
- How would you know if a student was receiving an appropriate educational program?
- What changes in education of students with disabilities have resulted from federal legal cases and legislation?

Introduction to
The Legal Foundations
of Special Education

Timothy was a 13-year-old with quadriplegia and severe mental retardation. He could hear and respond to words, music, and touching, but his school district in Rochester, New Hampshire, decided that he was not eligible for special education services because there was no indication that he would benefit from them. Basically, the school district thought he could not be educated, so there was no point in spending money on a program for him.

His parents and others disagreed, and a suit was filed on his behalf, alleging that his legal rights had been violated. In 1988, a U.S. District Court upheld the school district's decision. According to the court, federal law required school districts to determine first whether a child would benefit from special education; if the child would presumably show little or no benefit, no special education was necessary.

The next year, however, a federal appeals court reversed the decision (*Timothy W. v. Rochester, New Hampshire, School District*, 1989). Basing their decision on the 1975 Education for All Handicapped Children Act, the appeals court judges declared that all children with disabilities must receive an appropriate public education, regardless of the severity of the disabilities or the achievement level the children might be expected to attain. The judges sent the case back to the district court, demanding that the school district develop an individualized education program for Timothy.

(Continued)

(Continued)

> The decision created a good deal of controversy. Some people celebrated the ruling that federal law really meant what it said: All children with disabilities have the right to a free, appropriate public education. Others, however—especially public school officials—worried about the financial burden on public schools and on taxpayers.

A s the case of Timothy demonstrates, the courts and federal and state legislatures have become deeply involved in the process of special education since the early 1970s. Educators have been compelled to comply with an increasing number of court rulings and laws. In this process of change, the primary movers have been the parents of students with disabilities. Much of the legislation and most of the court rulings that have changed the practices of special education are a product of parents working to redress problems with the education their children were receiving. Parents have formed advocacy groups, acting on behalf of students with disabilities. For example, if a group of parents of children who are mentally retarded believe that their children are being excluded from school programs, the parents go to court to compel the schools to include the children. When many parents in many states start taking legal action on the same issue—such as the inclusion of children who are mentally retarded in public school classes—and when that action reflects a shift in public opinion, Congress may pass a law that addresses the parents' concerns. Over time, special education has undergone radical change as a result of such judicial and legislative actions.

Before 1975, when the Education for All Handicapped Children Act was passed, students with disabilities did not have the right to a free, appropriate public education. As a result, many students with severe disabilities were relegated to living at home with their parents, not attending school, and often not being taken out of the house. Others were placed in institutions where they were treated in a custodial manner. Staff attended to their physical needs, but they received little or no education. Today all students, including those with disabilities, have the right to a free, appropriate public education in a setting that is as much like general education as possible.

The Law Continues to Change

It is important to recognize that the situation is dynamic. People talk about the law, but the law is always changing. Practices that were followed yesterday may be illegal today. Procedures that are required today may be replaced by others tomorrow. Laws, rules, and regulations change as society's social and economic priorities change. Still, despite the evolutionary nature of the process, at any specific time the laws, practices, and procedures that govern education are expected to reflect the broad principles of freedom and equality that society, through the U.S. Constitution, has agreed on. As we write this text—even as you read it—U.S. Congress, state legislatures, and the courts are shaping public policy in special education by making and interpreting laws that affect how students are treated in our schools.

The Equal Protection Clause

The fundamental principle that underlies both litigation and legislation about the rights of students who are exceptional is the **equal protection clause** of the Fourteenth Amendment to the U.S. Constitution. The Fourteenth Amendment specifies that:

> no State shall make or enforce any law which shall abridge the privileges or immunities of citizens of the United States; nor shall any State deprive any person of life, liberty, or property, without due process of law;

nor deny to any person within its jurisdiction the *equal protection* of the laws.

It was the civil rights movement that pushed the equal protection clause onto national and state agendas. As court decisions and laws addressed the rights of people of color and women, the movement gradually expanded to protect the rights of people with disabilities. Today, schools are held accountable for demonstrating that they have educated all students, including those with disabilities.

1

Which Laws Affecting Special Education Should Every Teacher Know?

I f you asked 100 directors of special education why special education services exist in their school districts, more than half probably would answer that state and federal laws require them. If you asked specific questions—Why do you try to educate nondisabled students and students who have disabilities in the same classes? Why do you allow parents to challenge proposed changes in their child's educational program? Why do you make extensive efforts to conduct evaluations that are not racially or culturally biased? Why do school personnel write individualized education programs for students with disabilities?—most of the directors probably would say that state and federal laws require these actions. Most would also indicate that changes that have taken place in the education of students with disabilities, changes that have been in response to the courts or legislatures, have been for the good.

A BRIEF HISTORY

The history of legislation to provide services for people with disabilities dates back to 1817 with formation of the American

Asylum for the Education and Instruction of the Deaf. Before 1950, most laws were directed at providing institutional care or rehabilitative services. For example, in the 19th century, legislation was enacted to fund asylums, hospitals, and institutions for those with physical and mental disabilities. In the first half of the 20th century, laws were passed to support vocational rehabilitation for disabled war veterans and counseling and job placement for citizens with physical disabilities. In the 1950s, the focus of legislation began to change. Although state and community facilities continued to be funded, there was a new emphasis on research and training, vocational education, assessment, and special education services.

EIGHT IMPORTANT LAWS

Eight laws have important effects on the current practice of special education:

Section 504 of the Rehabilitation Act of 1973 (Public Law 93–112)

Education for All Handicapped Children Act of 1975 (Public Law 94–142)

1986 Amendments to the Education for All Handicapped Children Act (Public Law 99–457)

Individuals With Disabilities Education Act of 1990 (Public Law 101–476)

Americans With Disabilities Act of 1990 (Public Law 101–336)

Amendments to the Individuals With Disabilities Education Act (Public Law 105–17) of 1997

No Child Left Behind Act (Public Law 107–110) of 2001

Reauthorization of the Individuals With Disabilities Education Act of 2004 (IDEA)

Table 1.1 lists the major provisions of these laws.

Table 1.1   Major Federal Laws Affecting Special Education
and Their Key Provisions

Section 504 of the Rehabilitation Act (1973)

It is illegal to deny participation in activities, benefits of programs, or to in any way discriminate against a person with a disability solely because of that disability.

Individuals with disabilities must have equal access to programs and services.

Auxiliary aids must be provided to individuals with impaired speaking, manual, or sensory skills.

Education for All Handicapped Children Act (1975)

Students with disabilities have the right to a free, appropriate public education.

Schools must have on file an individualized education program for each student with a disability.

Parents have the right to inspect school records on their child, and when changes are made in a student's educational placement or program, parents must be informed. Parents have the right to challenge what is in records or to challenge changes in placement.

Students with disabilities have the right to be educated in the least restrictive educational environment.

Students with disabilities must be assessed in ways that are considered fair and nondiscriminatory. They have specific protections.

1986 Amendments to the Education for All Handicapped Children Act

Extends all rights of the Education for All Handicapped Children Act to preschoolers with disabilities

Requires each school district to conduct a multidisciplinary assessment and develop an individualized family service plan for each preschool child with a disability

(Continued)

Table 1.1 (Continued)

Individuals With Disabilities Education Act (1990)

Reauthorizes the Education for All Handicapped Children Act

Adds two new disability categories (traumatic brain injury and autism) to the definitions of students with disabilities

Adds a comprehensive definition of transition services

Includes provisions to make assistive technology more widely available

Americans With Disabilities Act (1992)

Prohibits discrimination on the basis of disability in employment, services rendered by state and local governments, places of public accommodation, transportation, and telecommunication services

Amendments to the Individuals With Disabilities Education Act (1997)

Specifies the participants of IEP teams and IEP documentation

Adds disciplinary changes to IDEA

Requires states to report on the performance and progress of all students

No Child Left Behind Act (2001)

Reauthorizes the Elementary and Secondary Education Act

Specifies that its provisions are for all students, including those with disabilities

Requires annual assessments in reading and math in Grades 3–8 and one year of high school

Provides for literacy interventions through Reading First and Early Reading First

Gives entitlement to supplementary education services

Allows increased parental flexibility in schools that are performing poorly (entitlement to change schools or school districts)

Individuals With Disabilities Education Improvement Act of 2004

Students with disabilities must be taught by highly qualified teachers who have full certification in special education or pass a state special education teacher licensing exam and hold a state license.

New approaches are permitted in identifying students as learning disabled.

Discrepancy scores are no longer required in identification of students with learning disabilities.

Fifteen percent of special education funds may go to providing support services in general education to students not yet identified as disabled.

Special education teachers teaching to alternate achievement standards in specific core academic subjects need to be certified in special education and the core academic subject.

Requirement of having benchmarks and short-term objectives in IEPs is deleted.

Development of multiple-year IEPs is allowed on a selective basis.

Transition planning must be results oriented.

Schools must appoint a parent surrogate for disabled students who are homeless or wards of the court.

Section 504 of the Rehabilitation Act

Section 504 of the Rehabilitation Act of 1973, which was finally adopted in 1977, prohibits discrimination against people with disabilities:

> No otherwise qualified handicapped individual shall, solely by reason of his handicap, be excluded from the participation in, be denied the benefits of, or be subjected to discrimination in any program or activity receiving federal financial assistance.

Because states and school districts depend, at least in part, on federal money to educate students with disabilities, most choose to comply with this mandate.

Equal Access

Another important provision of Section 504 is **architectural accessibility**—the removal of steps and other barriers that limit the participation of people with disabilities. The law does not require that every building be barrier free, or that every method of transportation be accessible to those who are disabled. Instead, it demands equal access to programs and services. For instance, a college does not have to make every building barrier free, but it does have to offer at least one section of every class in a building that is barrier free. If band concerts are held in only one building on campus, that building must be accessible to those who are disabled, so that they, like their nondisabled peers, have the opportunity to attend concerts. If the college does not make that building barrier free, any federal funds it receives can be cut off.

Auxiliary Aids

Section 504 also mandates the provision of auxiliary aids (readers for students who are blind, interpreters for students who are deaf) for those with impaired sensory, manual, or speaking skills. This does not mean that a school must provide these services at all times; it simply means that it cannot exclude students because it does not have an appropriate aid present.

Breadth of Coverage

Most of the provisions of Section 504 were incorporated into and expanded in the Education for All Handicapped Children Act of 1975 and later legislation. But Section 504 still serves a purpose because of its breadth of coverage: Its provisions are not restricted to a specific age group or to education. Section 504 is the law most often cited in court cases involving employment of people with disabilities and appropriate education in colleges and universities for students who are disabled. Also, the accessibility provisions of the law have removed the architectural barriers that limited the full participation of those with disabilities in school and community functions. Recently Section 504 has been used to get services for students who are said to have attention deficit disorder (ADD). Since ADD is not defined as a disability by the Individuals With Disabilities Education Act, Section 504 has once again played a major role.

Education for All Handicapped Children Act

On November 29, 1975, President Ford signed the **Education for All Handicapped Children Act**. This famous act is often cited simply by its number: **Public Law 94–142**. The law mandated *a free, appropriate public education* for students with disabilities between the ages of 3 and 21. It had four objectives:

1. Assure that all children with disabilities have available to them a free, appropriate public education.

2. Assure that the rights of children with disabilities and their parents are protected.

3. Assist states and localities to provide for the education of children with disabilities.

4. Assess and assure the effectiveness of efforts to educate children with disabilities.

Problems Addressed by Public Law 94–142

The Education for All Handicapped Children Act came about because parents, advocacy groups, and professionals were dissatisfied with certain conditions and brought them to the attention of legislators. Among other things, Congress found the following:

More than 8 million children with disabilities (from birth to age 21) were living in the United States, more than half of whom were not receiving an appropriate education.

More than 1 million children with disabilities were excluded entirely from the educational system, and many others were enrolled in regular education classes where, because their disabilities were undetected, they were not learning as much as could be expected.

Families were being forced to find services outside the public schools because the educational services within the schools were inadequate (U.S. Congress, 1975).

Lawmakers believed that special education could make a difference, that with special education services these children would stand a better chance of achieving their potential. They believed that it was in the national interest to fund programs to meet the needs of students who were disabled.

Specific Procedures

Public Law 94–142 set forth a number of procedures; states that did not comply with them would not receive federal funds. Specifically, the law required each state to have a plan that fully described the policies and procedures used to ensure a free, appropriate education for all students with disabilities between the ages of 3 and 21 and to have procedures in place for identifying all students with disabilities.

The law makes several very specific provisions for the education of students with disabilities. For example, whenever possible, they must be taught in general education classrooms, along with their nondisabled peers. Also, tests and other evaluation devices used to decide the nature of students' disabilities must be both racially and culturally fair. Although the "Protection in Evaluation Procedures" provisions of the law say that tests must be fair, "fairness" is not defined.

Four Provisions of the Law

Four specific areas of the law provide a perspective on the magnitude of this landmark legislation:

- Individualized education program (IEP)
- Due process

- Protection in evaluation procedures (PEP)
- Least restrictive environment (LRE)

As you read about each of these provisions, think about how they affect the work of special education teachers, general education teachers, school psychologists, administrators, counselors, speech-language pathologists, and all the other people who work with students who are exceptional. Think also about how it will affect your work to achieve maximum educational results for students who are exceptional.

Individualized Education Program (IEP)   A central concept to Public Law 94–142 is the **individualized education program (IEP)**. An IEP is a written document that describes:

- The student's present levels of functioning
- Annual goals and short-term objectives of the program
- Services to be provided and the extent of regular programming
- Starting date and expected duration of services
- Evaluation procedures and criteria for monitoring progress

Measurable Goals
An IEP is the product of a thorough evaluation that begins with information about the child gathered from parents, teachers, and formal and informal assessments, and often ends with a review by a team of professionals.

Public Law 94–142 states that the instructional goals specified in an IEP must be measurable, observable, and based on performance. *Figures 1.1a* and *1.1b* show the IEP of a fifth grader with learning disabilities in reading, math, and language skills. Notice that assessment results are specified, along with long- and short-term goals and a description of the services to be provided. In actual practice, the objectives are often written even more specifically, defining precise levels of desired achievement and ways they will be measured.

Reasons for IEPs
Why is such a formal plan necessary? What were lawmakers thinking when they drafted the IEP provision? First, lawmakers

Figure 1.1a

INDIVIDUALIZED EDUCATION PROGRAM

_11/11/05_

Date

STUDENT	Last Name	First	Middle	
			_5.3_	_8-4-95_
School of Attendance	Home School		Grade Level	Birthdate/Age

School Address   School Telephone Number

Child Study Team Members

LD Teacher

Case Manager

Homeroom		_Parents_	
Name	Title	Name	Title
Facilitator			
Name	Title	Name	Title
Speech			
Name	Title	Name	Title

Summary of Assessment Results

IDENTIFIED STUDENT NEEDS: _Reading from last half of DISTAR II –_

Present performance level

LONG-TERM GOALS: _To improve reading achievement level_
by at least one year's gain. To improve math achievement
to grade level. To improve language skills by one year's gain.

SHORT-TERM GOALS: _Master Level 4 vocabulary and reading_
skills. Master math skills in basic curriculum. Master spelling
words from level 3 list. Complete units 1 – 9 from level 3 curriculum.

White copy – Cumulative folder	Goldenrod copy – Case manager
Pink copy – Special teacher	Yellow copy – Parent

Figure 1.1b

Description of Services to Be Provided

Type of Service	Teacher	Starting Date	Amt. of time per day	OBJECTIVES AND CRITERIA FOR ATTAINMENT
SLD Level 999	*LD teacher*	*11 – 11 – 05*	*2½ hrs.*	*Reading: will know all vocabulary through the "Honeycomb" level. Will master skills as presented through DISTAR 99. Will know 123 sound-symbols presented in "Sound Way to Reading".* *Math: will pass all tests at basic 4 level.* *Spelling: 5 words each week from Level 3 list.* *Language: will complete Units 1–9 of the grade 4 language program. Will also complete supplemental units from "Language Step by Step".*

Mainstream Classes	Teacher	Amt. of time per day	OBJECTIVES AND CRITERIA FOR ATTAINMENT
		3½ hrs.	*Out-of-seat behavior: sit attentively and listen during mainstream class discussions. A simple management plan will be implemented if he does not meet this expectation. Mainstream modifications of Social Studies: will keep a folder in which he expresses through drawing the topics his class will cover. Modified district social studies curriculum. No formal testing will be made. An oral reader will read text to him, and oral questions will be asked.*

The following equipment, and other changes in personnel, transportation, curriculum, methods, and educational services will be made:

DISTAR 99 Reading Program, Spelling Level 3, "Sound Way to Reading"

Program, vocabulary tapes.

Substantiation of least restrictive alternatives:

The planning team has determined the student's academic needs are best met with direct SLD support in

reading, math, language, and spelling.

ANTICIPATED LENGTH OF PLAN *1 yr.*   The next periodic review will be held: *May 2005*

Date/Time/Place

☒   **I do approve this program placement and the above IEP**

☐   **I do not approve this placement and/or the IEP**   PARENT/GUARDIAN

☐   **I request a conciliation conference**   Principal or Designee

Source: Figure 1.1 reprinted from "Honig v. Doe: The Suspension and Expulsion of Handicapped Students" by M. L. Yell, *Exceptional Children*, vol. 56, pp. 60–69. Copyright © 1989 The Council for Exceptional Children. Reprinted with permission.

recognized the need for a mechanism to keep track of a student's progress. Second, special educators had convinced them that students would benefit more from their education if school personnel had specific objectives—a plan of where the student was going and how the student was going to get there—and a method for evaluating the extent to which the student was meeting individual goals.

The IEP has had a profound effect on the activities of teachers, school psychologists, and other school personnel. Students must be assessed by a multidisciplinary team (see *Figure 1.2*), and that assessment must form the basis of students' individualized educational programs. Their programs can then be carried out in a variety of settings (general education classes, self-contained classes, homes, and separate schools). Teachers (in both general and special education) are expected to provide instruction that ties in with the goals specified in the IEP.

Figure 1.2   IEP Team Members Required by the IDEA
Amendments

Parent(s)

Local education agency representative (who is qualified to provide special education services, able to commit school district resources, and able to ensure that the educational services specified in the IEP will be provided)

Student's special education teacher

Student's general education teacher

Professional who can interpret the instructional implications of evaluation results

Student, when appropriate

Others—at the discretion of parent(s) or school

Due Process The Fourteenth Amendment of the Constitution guarantees the citizens of the United States **due process** of law (e.g., the right to a fair trial, the right to be present at the trial). Public Law 94–142 reaffirms that guarantee for students with disabilities. The law gives parents, guardians, or parent surrogates the right to examine their children's records. It also gives them the right to independent evaluations of their children. At one time, the practice of testing children and making changes in their educational placement without parental knowledge or consent was widespread. Parents had little or no input in their children's education. The due process provisions of Public Law 94–142 bring parents into the system. Parents now have an opportunity to be involved, to understand and question what the schools are doing with their children.

Prior Written Notice

Whenever a school proposes or refuses to change the identification, evaluation, or placement of a child, the parents must receive prior written notice (in their native language, if at all possible). Parents have the right to challenge the school's decision at an impartial hearing. If the parents are not satisfied with the findings of the hearing, in most states they can appeal the decision to the state education agency, and from there to the civil courts.

Due Process Hearing

At a due process hearing, parents have the right to:

Counsel and/or experts in special education

Present evidence, cross-examine, and compel the attendance of witnesses

Receive a written or taped record of the hearing

These due process rights apply whether the hearing is in an educational facility or in a court.

Protection in Evaluation Procedures (PEP) The **protection in evaluation procedures (PEP)** provisions of Public Law 94–142 address assessment practices. Assessment practices must be fair, with no racial or cultural bias. This provision was put in place because it was thought that students who were inappropriately assessed would be inappropriately placed. It was thought that they could end up in "dead end" placements, be stigmatized, and have limited life opportunities if they were assessed with tests that were not fair.

School personnel must provide state education agency personnel with assurance that they are using fair (unbiased) testing and evaluation materials to decide whether students are disabled and to decide where students will receive their educational programs. Tests must be selected and administered in ways that are not racially and culturally discriminatory. There are specific rules and regulations for the implementation of the PEP provisions:

> A "full and individual evaluation" of a student's needs must be made before the student is placed in a special education program.
>
> Tests must be administered in the child's native language or other mode of communication.
>
> Tests must be valid for the specific purpose for which they are used.
>
> Tests must be administered by trained personnel following the instructions provided by their developer.
>
> Tests and other evaluation materials must be relevant to specific areas of educational needs, not designed to yield a single general IQ (intelligence quotient) score.
>
> The results of tests administered to students who have impaired sensory, manual, or speaking skills must reflect aptitude or achievement, not the impairment.
>
> Special education placement cannot be determined on the basis of a single procedure. More than one test must be used.
>
> Evaluations for special education placement must be made by a multidisciplinary team, including at least one teacher or other specialist with "knowledge in the area of [the] suspected disability."

Students must be assessed in all areas related to their suspected disability, including general health, vision, hearing, behavior, general intelligence, motor abilities, academic performance, and language abilities.

The PEP provisions were included in Public Law 94–142 to address abuses in the assessment process. In the background testimony for this law, parents asserted that their children were being tested with unfair tests—tests that were in languages other than their primary languages and that included items from cultures other than those to which the children had been exposed. It was argued that a law should be enacted to stop these abuses. The product was the PEP provisions.

Least Restrictive Environment   Public Law 94–142 specifies that students who are disabled be educated in the **least restrictive environment (LRE)**. States must have policies and procedures in place to ensure that students with disabilities, including those in public or private institutions or other care facilities, are educated with students who are not disabled. States must also ensure that students are removed from the general education environment only when a disability is severe enough that instruction in general education classes with the use of supplementary aids and services is not effective.

The LRE provisions reflect the generally held belief that students are better off and demonstrate better development when they spend as much time as possible interacting with their nondisabled peers. If students can learn in an environment that is relatively nonrestrictive, then they can live and work in that environment as they get older. The LRE provision is sometimes referred to as the **mainstreaming** provision because it specifies that students must be educated in the mainstream of education to the fullest possible extent.

The Three-Stage Process and Public Law 94–142

The intent of Public Law 94–142 was massive educational reform for students with disabilities. Its major provisions target each stage of the decision-making process. This process can be broken into three distinct stages in which educators decide:

1. Whom to serve (determining eligibility)

2. How to serve those students (treatment practices)

3. Whether the services have been of benefit (progress evaluation)

The due process and PEP provisions relate to the first stage, determining eligibility. They attempt to assist school personnel in making decisions about who should receive special education. The IEP and LRE provisions target the second stage, treatment practices. The intent is to specify precisely the nature of the educational program that will be provided, where it will be provided, and by whom. All the provisions address aspects of progress evaluation, the third stage of the process.

Of course, passing a law does not guarantee that changes will occur in the ways the law directs. Interpretation of the law— by the courts—influences the effect the law has on practice.

Amendments to the Education for All Handicapped Children Act

In 1986 Congress amended Public Law 94–142 by passing **Public Law 99–457** (the amendments to the Education for All Handicapped Children Act). This law extended all rights and protections of the law to preschoolers with disabilities. Effective in the 1990–1991 academic year, all states that applied for funds under Public Law 94–142 had to provide free, appropriate public education to all children with disabilities aged 3 through 5.

At the same time, as part of Public Law 99–457, Congress established a new state grant program for infants and toddlers with disabilities. Eligible for **early intervention** are children from birth through age 2 who are delayed in development or at risk of substantial delay in development. The states have the authority to specify the criteria for deciding whom to serve.

To receive the federal funds available as part of Public Law 99–457, a state must have an agency that administers the services and an interagency coordinating council to help develop programs and services. State early intervention programs are required to provide all eligible infants and toddlers with multidisciplinary assessments, individualized programs, and case management services.

Individualized Family Service Plans (IFSPs)

As part of the early intervention program, the law specifies that each school district use a multidisciplinary assessment to develop an **individualized family service plan (IFSP)** for each child. IFSPs are contracts between families and schools that provide agreement on the kinds of services students will receive. It gives families assurance of services. The IFSP functions much like an IEP but includes a description of the family's needs and services as well as those of the child. The IFSP must state:

The child's present level of cognitive, social, speech and language, and self-help development

Family strengths and needs related to enhancing the child's development

Major outcomes expected for the child and family

Criteria, procedures, and timelines for measuring progress

Specific early intervention services necessary to meet the unique needs of the child and family, including methods, frequency, and intensity of service

Projected dates for initiation and expected duration of services

Name of the person who will manage the case

Procedures for transition from early intervention into a preschool program

Individuals With Disabilities Education Act (IDEA)

The 1990 **Individuals With Disabilities Education Act (IDEA)**, Public Law 101–476, is a reauthorization of the Education for All Handicapped Children Act. It reaffirmed a national intent to support appropriate education for students with special learning needs. To reflect contemporary practices, the law replaced references to "handicapped children" with "children with disabilities." Two new disability categories (autism and traumatic brain injury) were added to the definition of "children with disabilities," and a comprehensive definition of **transition services** (services to ensure smooth movement from school to post-school activities) was added. The law also specified that schools must develop **individualized transition plans (ITPs)** for students 16 years of age or older.

Assistive Technologies

IDEA further states that students with disabilities should have access to assistive technology equipment and associated services, including purchasing or leasing technological devices and training in their use. Calculators for students with learning disabilities, closed-captioned television systems for students with hearing impairments, electronic communication aids for students with speech or language disorders—all of these are examples of assistive technology supplied under IDEA guidelines. Decisions about a student's need for assistive technology are generally made by the team that develops the IEP.

Americans With Disabilities Act

The purpose of the **Americans With Disabilities Act (ADA)** of 1990, Public Law 101–336, is to extend to people with disabilities civil rights similar to those now available on the basis of race, color, national origin, gender, and religion through the Civil Rights Act (1964). ADA prohibits discrimination on the basis of disability in:

Employment

Services rendered by state and local governments

Places of public accommodation, transportation, and telecommunication services (e.g., phones)

Under ADA, employers cannot discriminate against individuals with disabilities. They must use employment application procedures that enable individuals with disabilities to apply for jobs; in making decisions about whom to hire, advance, or discharge, employers are not allowed to do so on the basis of disability; individuals with disabilities should not be paid differently from others, they have the same rights to job training, and they are to have the same privileges of employment as others.

Amendments to IDEA

In 1997, **Public Law 105–17** reauthorized and extended some aspects of IDEA. The intent of these amendments was to increase parental participation in the evaluation process, placement decisions, and program planning for students with disabilities. The IDEA amendments made two major changes to the formal three-year reevaluation process: prior parental consent and a streamlined process. In addition, the amendments revised membership of IEP teams and content of IEPs and clarified discipline policies for students with disabilities.

Parental Consent to Reevaluation

Under the IDEA Amendments, parents must consent before a complete reevaluation can proceed. Schools must strive to acquire parental consent before beginning the reevaluation process in which placement decisions are examined.

Streamlined Reevaluation

The second major change the IDEA Amendments made to the reevaluation process is a streamlining of the periodic reevaluation that is undertaken every three years. This change was made in order to reduce the need for a complete reevaluation. If the IEP team is able to make the decision for continued eligibility based on existing information and prior results, then they may forego the complete battery of testing. This does not obviate the need for a full reevaluation because the team may decide that this will be in the best interest of the student.

IEP Team Composition

In addition to reevaluation changes, the 1997 IDEA Amendments made changes to the IEP process. The first change to the IEP process addressed the need for specific expertise to be included in the IEP team. A general education teacher must now be present and participate in most aspects of the IEP team meetings. In addition, one of the members of the team must have knowledge and expertise in evaluation and be able to translate evaluation results into instructional objectives.

The purpose of the IEP team changes is to involve the general education teacher more fully in the planning and to provide a link between evaluation results and instructional objectives and interventions.

IEP Content

The IDEA Amendments changed the required content of IEP documentation as well, signaling a movement toward greater accountability. According to the amendments, the IEP must now contain *measurable* goals, and parents must receive a progress report as often as parents of students in general education. Also, students with disabilities must be included in district and statewide assessment systems, and their test results must be reported along with all other reporting mechanisms. This is one of the most important accountability controls that has been mandated.

Discipline Policies

The IDEA amendments strive to balance the school district's obligation to provide a safe, structured learning environment with the obligation to provide students with disabilities a fair and appropriate public education. In terms of discipline, the amendments allow schools to discipline a student with a disability similarly to a student without a disability, with a few exceptions:

> First, if a student with a disability is suspended or has had a disciplinary procedure that constitutes a change of placement for more than ten school days during a school year, the school must provide educational services during that time.

> Second, a student with a disability may be removed from the school and placed in an interim alternative educational setting if he or she brings a weapon to school or a school function or if he or she solicits the sale of illegal drugs at school or at a school function.

> Third, the school may request an expedited hearing with a hearing officer if the school has concerns about the student's potential risk to others.

The amendments also specify that a **manifestation determination** be conducted within ten days of any action that would constitute a change in placement for greater than ten cumulative school days. A manifestation determination is an inquiry into whether a student's misbehavior was related to his or her disability. If there is a relationship, the student can be neither suspended for more than 10 days nor expelled. If there is no relationship, the student may be disciplined in the same manner as a student without disabilities, including long-term suspension or expulsion (Yell, 1989, p. 66). For a manifestation determination, all available information is gathered in order to determine if there is a relationship between the offensive action and the student's disability. The parents of the student may request an expedited due process hearing if they disagree with the results of the determination team or if they feel that due process procedures were not implemented correctly.

No Child Left Behind Act

The Elementary and Secondary Education Act (ESEA), a fundamental federal law specifying the nature of education that must be provided to students, was reauthorized in 2001 and is now commonly referred to as the No Child Left Behind Act

(Public Law 107–110). This law has as its foundation four pillars of President George W. Bush's educational reform agenda: accountability for results, focus on proven (through scientific research) educational methods, state and local flexibility, and expanded choices for families. The key provisions of the act include:

Rigorous academic standards

Annual assessments in reading and mathematics in Grades 3–8, plus one high school grade

Accountability (adequate yearly progress and improvement/corrective action/restructuring)

Parental choice (transfer to better public schools, supplemental educational services—public or private, more charter schools)

Educator quality

New programs (including Reading First and Early Reading First)

Strong emphasis on scientific research

The No Child Left Behind Act is a general education act. Yet, it is extremely important for the education of students with disabilities because it specifies that its provisions are for *all* students, including students with disabilities and students with limited English proficiency.

At the time of this writing, the No Child Left Behind Act (which was issued and commented on) is being rewritten. This law will strengthen accountability programs by including all students. School personnel will need to include students with disabilities in their accountability systems. The law will also include a major preventive component. Extensive services in reading are to be put in place in poverty schools (where many students experience reading difficulties).

Reading First

Part of the Elementary and Secondary School Act was President Clinton's Reading Excellence Act. Likewise, the academic cornerstone of No Child Left Behind is Reading First. This legislation is designed to get all students reading by the end of third grade. The Early Reading First legislation provides for preschool interventions for students from poverty schools. It is designed to prevent reading difficulties and enhance competence in early literacy. The No Child Left Behind Act also gives students from poverty schools the right to private tutoring. In addition, it affords students from schools that are failing the right to enroll in charter schools. Clearly, this law impacts the education of students with disabilities.

2004 Reauthorization of IDEA

The Individuals With Disabilities Education Act (IDEA) was reauthorized by Congress in November 2004 and signed into law by the President on December 3, 2004. This reauthorization is sometimes referred to as H.B. 1350 (House Bill 1350). A number of changes were made to IDEA, and many of the changes were made in an effort to bring the language and requirements of the No Child Left Behind Act into closer agreement with the language and requirements of IDEA. For one thing, Congress changed the name of the law to the Individuals with Disabilities Education Improvement Act to reflect the shift in focus from compliance to improved educational outcomes. Remember that many practice requirements of laws are derived from specification of rules and guidelines. At the time we prepared this book, the federal government was beginning hearings across the nation that are the necessary and required prerequisite to writing of the rules and guidelines. We expect that it will take until at least mid-2006 before the rules and regulations are written and undergo a required period of public comment.

"Highly Qualified Teacher"

The law now specifies that students with disabilities are to be taught by highly qualified teachers who have full certification in special education or who pass a state special education teacher licensing exam and hold a state license. The law elaborates on this provision by specifying a push for high-quality, intensive preservice preparation and professional development for all personnel who work with students with disabilities. A new requirement is that those who teach core content subjects (English and language arts, math, science) to students with disabilities must also hold certification in the content areas they teach. Thus, a high school teacher who teaches math to students with disabilities will need to be dually certified in math and special education or will need to be certified in math and pass a state examination in special education. Special education teachers teaching to alternate achievement standards in specific core academic subjects also need to be certified in special education and the core academic subject.

New Approaches to Identifying Students as Learning Disabled

In reauthorizing IDEA, Congress removed the requirement that schools show that students they identify as learning disabled have a discrepancy between ability and achievement. The law states that schools "shall not be required to take into consideration whether a child has a severe discrepancy between achievement and intellectual ability in oral expression, listening comprehension, written expression, basic reading skill, reading comprehension, math calculation, or mathematical reasoning." The law goes on to say that the school may use a process that determines if the child responds to scientific research-based intervention as a part of the evaluation procedures.

Assessment in Native Language or Mode of Communication

Congress removed the requirement that a student be assessed in his or her native language. It replaced this requirement with the statement that assessments should be "administered in the language and form most likely to yield accurate information on what the child knows and can do academically, developmentally and functionally unless not feasible to provide and administer." This provision was inserted into the law in recognition of the fact that students whose native language is a language other than English are at different points developmentally in their knowledge and use of English, and that a test in the native language or mode of communication may not always be the best and most appropriate way to get information needed to plan appropriate educational programs.

Provision of Special Education Services to Students in General Education

Up to 15 percent of IDEA funds can be used for general education support services for students who are not yet identified as disabled. This enables school personnel to beef up preventive and prereferral services.

IEP Provisions

Several changes were made to IEP requirements. First, Congress required that educational professionals specify benchmarks and short-term objectives for students with disabilities who take alternate assessments aligned to alternate achievement standards. Also, Congress removed this requirement for IEPs for students who are disabled but working toward the same state standards as nondisabled students. Now school personnel must specify annual academic and functional goals for students with disabilities. At the same time, Congress added the requirement that IEP teams indicate how progress toward annual goals will be measured and when progress will be reported. Finally, Congress added the requirement that the instruction specified in IEPs should be evidence-based instruction that is based on peer-reviewed research to the extent practicable.

Transition Planning

Congress added language to the transition planning requirements of IDEA. It is now specified that transition planning is to be a "results-oriented" process focused on improving academic and functional achievement.

Homeless Children or Those Who Are Wards of the Court

Congress addressed the fact that some children with disabilities are wards of the court or are homeless and that there are occasions on which the school does not know who the child's parents are. Schools are now required to appoint a parent surrogate for children who are wards of the court, unaccompanied homeless children, or those for whom the parents are unknown. Congress also specified that the parent surrogate could not be an employee of the state or local education agency or of an agency that provides services to the child.

2

Which Court Cases Have Had the Most Impact on Special Education?

The laws we have described have brought about a revolution in special education since 1975. Much of the impetus behind these laws came from court cases, especially those brought by parents to challenge existing education practices. Even after the passage of a law, its effect often depends on the way the courts interpret it. For this reason, understanding the legal basis of special education requires some knowledge of major court rulings, as well as the understanding that courts are continuing to interpret and reinterpret the laws every year. Some of the most important court cases that have influenced special education are listed in *Table 2.1*.

BROWN V. BOARD OF EDUCATION

Court action before the enactment of Public Law 94–142 in 1975 focused on the individual's right to a free, appropriate public education and on guidelines for the states to follow in educating

(text continues on page 44)

Table 2.1   Influential Court Cases in Special Education

Year	Case	State	Ruling
1893	Watson v. City of Cambridge	Massachusetts	Students may be expelled for "disorderly conduct or imbecility."
1919	Beattie v. State Board of Education	Wisconsin	Students with physical disabilities may be excluded from school when their presence has a "depressing and nauseating effect" on other students.
1954	Brown v. Board of Education	Kansas	Segregation of schools is illegal because it denies equal protection and equal opportunity (U.S. Supreme Court).
1967	Hobson v. Hansen	Washington, DC	Ability grouping (tracking) based on performance on standardized tests—as employed by Washington, DC, schools—is unconstitutional, violating both due process and equal protection.
1969	Tinker v. Des Moines Independent Community	Iowa	Children are "persons" under the Constitution and have civil

Year	Case	State	Ruling
	School District		rights independent of their parents (U.S. Supreme Court).
1970	Diana v. State Board of Education	California	In a consent decree, the state agreed to:

Test all students whose primary language is not English in both their primary language and in English.

Eliminate from tests any "unfair verbal items."

Develop intelligence tests that reflect Mexican American culture and that are standardized only on students who are Mexican American.

Reevaluate all Mexican American and Chinese American students enrolled in classes for the educable mentally retarded using only nonverbal items and test them in their primary languages. |

(Continued)

(Continued)

Year	Case	State	Ruling
1971	Covarrubias v. San Diego Unified School District	California	A consent decree establishes the right of plaintiffs to monetary damages for misclassification.
1971	Lemon v. Bossier Parish School Board	Louisiana	Ability grouping is unconstitutional.
1971, 1972, 1974	Wyatt v. Stickney	Alabama	Students with mental retardation who are committed to state schools have a right to adequate treatment (education).
1972	Larry P. v. Riles	California	• The California State Department of Education cannot use intelligence tests to place students who are black in classes for students who are educable mentally retarded (EMR). • California schools must eliminate the disproportionate placement of students who are black in EMR classes.

Year	Case	State	Ruling
			• California schools must reevaluate all students who are black who are enrolled in EMR classes.
1974	Hairston v. Drosick	West Virginia	Exclusion of students with disabilities from the general education classroom without procedural safeguards is a violation of their constitutional rights as well as a violation of the Rehabilitation Act of 1973.
1975	Goss v. Lopez	Ohio	Due process is required before students are suspended or expelled from school (U.S. Supreme Court).
1976	Washington v. Davis	Washington, DC	When actions result in a discriminatory outcome, one can assume discriminatory intent (U.S. Supreme Court).
1976, 1977	Frederick L. v. Thomas	Pennsylvania	Philadelphia schools must engage in massive screening

(Continued)

(Continued)

Year	Case	State	Ruling
			and follow-up evaluations designed to locate and serve students with learning disabilities.
1977	Panitch v. State of Wisconsin	Wisconsin	A long delay in implementing a state law designed to give equal protection to those with disabilities is sufficient indication of "intentional discrimination," in violation of the equal protection clause.
1978	Lora v. New York City Board of Education	New York	• The process of evaluating students to determine if they should enter "special day schools" for students who are emotionally disturbed violates students' rights to treatment and due process. • To the extent that students are referred to largely racially segregated schools, there is a

Year	Case	State	Ruling
			denial of equal opportunity. • New York City's monetary problems do not excuse violation of students' rights.
1980	PASE v. Hannon	Illinois	Intelligence tests are not biased against students who are black and so are appropriate for use in placing students who are black in EMR classes. (This ruling contrasts with *Larry P. v. Riles*.)
1982	Hendrick Hudson District Board of Education v. Rowley	New York	It is not necessary for school districts to provide sign-language interpreters in classrooms as part of deaf students' education programs. Schools do not have to develop the maximum potential of students with disabilities; but they must grant them access to educational opportunities (U.S. Supreme Court).

(Continued)

(Continued)

Year	Case	State	Ruling
1984	Irving Independent School District v. Tatro	Texas	School personnel must provide related services that enable a student who is disabled to remain at school during the day (U.S. Supreme Court).
1984	Smith v. Robinson	Rhode Island	Attorneys' fees are not reimbursable under Public Law 94–142 (U.S. Supreme Court).
1985	Burlington School Committee v. Massachusetts Department of Education	Massachusetts	Reimbursement for private school tuition is an appropriate form of relief for a court to grant (U.S. Supreme Court).
1988	Honig v. Doe	California	Schools cannot unilaterally decide to expel or suspend students with disabilities (U.S. Supreme Court).
1989	Timothy W. v. Rochester, New Hampshire, School District	New Hampshire	All children with disabilities must be provided with educational programs, regardless of the severity of the disability and

Year	Case	State	Ruling
			regardless of whether educators predict the child will benefit from education.
1993	Zobrest v. Catalina Foothills School District	California	There is no general prohibition against providing special education services in parochial schools. The services must be provided in a religiously neutral manner, and IDEA funds must not find their way into the parochial school coffers.
1994	Light v. Parkway School District	Missouri	Disruptive students with disabilities do not actually have to cause harm before removal from school; rather, they have to be judged substantially likely to cause harm.
1996	Cefalu v. East Baton Rouge Parish School Board	Louisiana	A school district is not required to provide a sign-language interpreter at a parochial school; a school district offering free,

(Continued)

(Continued)

Year	Case	State	Ruling
			appropriate public education is under no further obligation to parent-placed, private school students with disabilities.
2002	Kevin T. v. Elmhurst Community School District No. 205	Illinois	If a district has failed to provide a free, appropriate public education and has graduated a student, it must continue to pay for the student's education after graduation and until age 22.

students. The cornerstone of this litigation was set in 1954, when the U.S. Supreme Court, in *Brown v. Board of Education,* ruled that separate schools for black and white students are inherently unequal and therefore unconstitutional. The parents of students with disabilities who later sued school systems for the denial of equal protection—complaining that their children had been assessed inaccurately or had been placed in inferior educational settings—based their legal arguments on the decision in *Brown.*

THE MANY ISSUES
ADDRESSED BY THE COURTS

The other issues the courts addressed before passage of Public Law 94–142 include:

Ability grouping based on test performance

The notion that children are persons under the Constitution and have civil rights

Exclusion of students with disabilities from schools

Misclassification of children who are nonwhite or non-English speaking

In separate cases, the courts ruled that:

The exclusion of students with behavior problems, mental retardation, emotional disturbance, or hyperactivity is unconstitutional.

It is illegal to group students by ability ("track") based on their performance on standardized tests.

All children with disabilities have the right to a "constructive" education.

Assessment tests must be in a student's primary language (in California).

Students who are mentally retarded have the right to attend schools with students who are not retarded.

SUPREME COURT RULINGS

In this section we focus on five U.S. Supreme Court cases. The Supreme Court has been involved in defining and clarifying the meaning of "appropriate education" as mandated by Section 601c of Public Law 94–142.

Access to Educational Opportunities

In *Hendrick Hudson District Board of Education v. Rowley* (1982), the Supreme Court overturned a lower-court ruling that had required a school to provide an interpreter for a deaf student. The case began when Amy Rowley's parents asked the school to provide a sign-language interpreter in their deaf daughter's class on a full-time basis. The school was providing speech therapy, use of a hearing aid, and a tutor for one hour a day, and had offered sign-language instruction to those of Amy's teachers who wanted it. But the school refused to put an interpreter in Amy's classroom. The Supreme Court ruled that the school was acting within its rights. In writing the decision for the Court, Justice William Rehnquist stated that schools do not have to develop the maximum potential of students with disabilities; the law was intended only to give students access to educational opportunities.

Enabling Students to Remain at School

In *Irving Independent School District v. Tatro* (1984), the issue was the responsibility of a school to provide a medical procedure, in this case catheterization, to a child with a disability. Chief Justice Warren Burger, writing for the majority, reasoned that:

> a service that enables a handicapped child to remain at school during the day is an important means of providing the child with the meaningful access to education that Congress envisioned. . . . Services like [catheterization] that permit a child to remain at school during the day are not less related to the effort to educate than are services that enable the child to reach, enter, or exist in the school. (*Irving Independent School District v. Tatro*, 1984)

Burger went on to say that services like catheterization, which can be carried out by a school nurse, must be provided by public schools.

Use of Private Schools

A third case heard by the Supreme Court involved the payment by school districts of private school tuition and fees for students who are disabled. In *Burlington School Committee v. Massachusetts Department of Education* (1985), the lower courts asked the Supreme Court for a ruling on the meaning of appropriate education. Michael Panaco, a first grader with a specific learning disability, was enrolled in a private school because his parents contended that he was not receiving an education that met his unique needs in the local public school. The Court noted that:

> where a court determines that a private placement desired by the parents was proper under the Act and that an IEP calling for placement in a public school was inappropriate, it seems clear beyond cavil that appropriate relief include[s] . . . placing the child in a private school. (*Burlington School Committee v. Massachusetts Department of Education*, 1985)

The Court ruled that the most important element of Public Law 94–142 is an appropriate educational program, wherever it takes place, and that the school district may be obliged to pay for private schooling.

Legal Fees

Court actions take time. For example, the *Burlington* case took eight years. They also cost a lot of money. Parents who go to court on behalf of their children incur extensive legal fees. It is not surprising, then, that the fourth case heard by the Supreme Court involved the issue of responsibility for legal fees. In *Smith v. Robinson* (1984), the school district had agreed to place Thomas Smith, a youngster with cerebral palsy and physical and emotional disabilities, in a day treatment program at a hospital in Rhode Island. Later the school district informed the parents that the Rhode Island Department of Mental Health, Retardation, and Hospitals would have to take over the expense of the program. The state supreme court ruled that the duty of funding the educational program rested with the local school, not the state. The parents appealed the case to a federal district court and, in addition, asked for payment of attorneys' fees. The district court agreed with the parents, but the court of appeals did not. The Supreme Court ruled that parents are responsible for paying attorneys' fees.

Bringing Learning to Life:
A Simple Medical Procedure

Amber Tarro was a child with spina bifida, a congenital disability in which the spinal column is imperfectly closed. To avoid damage to her kidneys, Amber needed a regular medical procedure known as clean intermittent catheterization (CIC), which involves washing a small metal tube called a catheter, inserting it in the bladder to allow urine to drain, pulling the catheter out, and wiping the area. This is a fairly simple procedure that can be done by a person with only minimal training; Amber's parents, her teenage brother, and her babysitter all performed CIC for her.

Her school district, however, refused to include CIC as part of Amber's IEP. CIC was a medical service, according to the school district, not a "related" service as required by Public Law 94–142. Amber's parents protested; they pointed out that by not offering CIC, the school district was essentially excluding Amber from school.

The argument ended up in the court system, where it eventually reached the U.S. Supreme Court. The Supreme Court distinguished between medical services that require a doctor and those that can be performed by a school nurse. Schools do not have to offer medical treatment by a physician. But since the school nurse could readily perform Amber's CIC, the Court ruled that it was indeed a "related" service and the school district was legally required to provide it.

So the Supreme Court had ruled that parents could be reimbursed for private school tuition but not for attorneys' fees. In 1986 Congress settled the issue by passing the **Handicapped Children's Protection Act** (1986), an amendment to Public Law 94–142. The amendment specified that courts could award attorneys' fees to parents who win in current proceedings or in cases that began after July 4, 1984 (coincidentally, this is the date that the rulings in both *Tatro* and *Smith* were read by the Supreme Court). Parents now have the right to collect attorneys' fees.

However, they must work in good faith to try to settle their case. Also, there are specific conditions under which parents are not entitled to recover attorneys' fees.

Exclusion of Students With Disabilities

In *Honig v. Doe* (1988), the Supreme Court reaffirmed the decision of a lower court that schools cannot exclude students with disabilities, specifically those who have emotional disturbances, because of their behavior. The case involved the suspension of two students who were receiving special education services in California's San Francisco School District. The students (called John Doe and Jack Smith in the decision) had been expelled for different reasons:

> Student Doe had been placed in a developmental center for handicapped students. While attending school, he assaulted another student and broke a window. When he admitted these offenses to the principal he was suspended for five days. The principal referred the matter to the school's student placement committee with the recommendation that Doe be expelled. The suspension was continued indefinitely as permitted by California state law, which allowed suspensions to extend beyond five days while expulsion proceedings were being held.

> Student Smith's individualized education program (IEP) stated he was to be placed in a special education program in a regular school setting on a trial basis. Following several incidences of misbehavior the school unilaterally reduced his program to half-day. His grandparents agreed to the reduction; however, the school district did not notify them of their right to appeal. A month later Smith was suspended for five days when he made inappropriate sexual comments to female students. In accordance with California law Smith's suspension was also continued indefinitely while expulsion proceedings were initiated by the school placement committee. (Yell, 1989, p. 64)

The case went through several courts, eventually ending up in the Supreme Court. Justice William Brennan, writing for the majority, stated that schools cannot unilaterally exclude disabled students. When placement is being debated, the student must remain in the current educational setting unless school officials and parents agree otherwise. The decision left a number of questions unanswered (Yell, 1989): In what ways can handicapped students be disciplined? How should the schools deal with students who are a danger to themselves or others but whose parents do not consent to removal?

3

The Legal Foundations of Special Education in Perspective

C onstitutional provisions, legislation, and litigation have
had a tremendous impact on the field of special education.
Much of current practice in the field has been shaped by them.
Changes in special education practice are less a product of new
teaching techniques, new research findings, and new technologies than a product of new laws and interpretations of those
laws.

What effect does this legal basis have on those who work
with exceptional students? As a practical matter, most of the
changes have meant more work for special educators: keeping
detailed records, filling out forms, meeting with other team
members. Another effect is the legal responsibilities that have
been attached not only to school districts and schools, but also
to educators.

FINDING A BALANCE

The lawmaking process draws on all kinds of information
and opinion in the drafting of new legislation. New teaching

techniques and research findings and technologies are examined. Parents, educators, and psychologists are heard. The end product attempts to find a balance between earlier practice and ideal possibility, attained through common sense and common decency. That product—the laws that shape special education— has immeasurably improved the delivery of special services to exceptional students.

4

What Have We Learned?

As you complete your study of the legal foundations of special education, it may be helpful to review what you have learned. To help you check your understanding, we have listed the key points and key vocabulary for you to review. We have included the Self-Assessment again so you can compare what you know now with what you knew as you began your study. Finally, we provide a few topics for you to think about and some activities for you to do "on your own."

KEY POINTS

▣ Federal and state laws, combined with a number of important court cases, have brought major changes in special education.

▣ The equal protection clause of the U.S. Constitution underlies much of the legal framework for special education.

▣ Major federal laws governing special education include Section 504 of the Rehabilitation Act (1973), the Education for All Handicapped Children Act (1975), the 1986

Amendments to the Education for All Handicapped Children Act, the Individuals With Disabilities Education Act of 1990 (IDEA), the Americans With Disabilities Act of 1990 (ADA), the 1997 Amendments to IDEA, and the 2004 Reauthorization of IDEA.

▣ The No Child Left Behind Act specifies that its provisions apply to all students, including those with disabilities and those with limited English proficiency.

▣ Federal laws require a free, appropriate public education for all children with disabilities. For each student who has a disability, educators must develop an individualized education program (IEP). Providers of early intervention are required to create an individualized family service plan (IFSP).

▣ Students with disabilities must be educated in the least restrictive environment (LRE); in practice, this often leads to mainstreaming (or inclusion), that is, educating students with disabilities in general education classrooms as much as possible.

▣ Federal laws guarantee due process for students and their parents and require that evaluation be conducted in a fair and nondiscriminatory manner.

▣ Court rulings have helped to define the educational services that meet the requirement of "appropriate" education. The U.S. Supreme Court has determined, for example, that schools must provide simple medical procedures that can be administered by a school nurse and that school districts must pay for private schooling when no appropriate public schooling is available.

KEY VOCABULARY

Architectural accessibility refers to the removal of steps and other barriers that limit the participation of people with disabilities.

Due process is provision of opportunity for a fair hearing before a change is made in educational placement.

Early intervention consists of educational and other treatment provided before a child reaches school age or before school-related problems become serious.

Equal protection clause is a provision of the Fourteenth Amendment to the U.S. Constitution providing that no state shall deprive any person of life, liberty, or property without due process of the law, nor deny any person equal protection of the laws.

FAPE is the acronym used to refer to a free and appropriate public education, a mandated right of individuals with disabilities.

Handicapped Children's Protection Act is an amendment to the original Education for All Handicapped Children Act specifying that courts could award attorneys' fees to parents who brought lawsuits.

Individualized education program (IEP) is a written document that includes (1) a statement of the student's present level of functioning, (2) a statement of annual goals and short-term objectives for achieving those goals, (3) a statement of services to be provided and the extent of regular programming, (4) the starting date and expected duration of services, and (5) evaluation procedures and criteria for monitoring progress.

Individualized family service plan (IFSP) is a term used to refer to a document used in an early intervention program to specify the child's level of current development and the family needs related to that development, objectives of the program, specific services that will be provided to the child and to the family, evaluation procedures, and transition procedures to move the child from early intervention into a preschool program.

Individualized transition plan (ITP) is a plan specifying actions that are to be taken to facilitate a smooth transition of a student from school to post-school activities like employment, employment in a sheltered workshop, living in a group home, or attending college or technical school.

Individuals With Disabilities Education Act (IDEA) is the name of the primary current federal law mandating a free and appropriate education to all individuals with disabilities.

Least restrictive environment (LRE) is an educational setting that is as much like the regular classroom as possible.

Mainstreaming refers to keeping exceptional students in regular classrooms and normal settings.

Manifestation determination consists of an inquiry into whether a student's misbehavior was related to or due to his or her disability.

Protection in evaluation procedures (PEP) are those provisions of IDEA that mandate nonbiased assessment procedures.

Public Law 94–142 is the legal name given to the Education for All Handicapped Children's Act of 1975.

Section 504 of the Rehabilitation Act was the first federal law prohibiting discrimination in employment against individuals solely on the basis of a disability.

Transition services refer to those special education services that enhance the transition of students from preschool to kindergarten, from school to work, or from one educational setting to another.

Self-Assessment 2

After you complete this book, check your knowledge and understanding of the content covered. Choose the best answer for each of the following questions.

1. The fundamental principle that underlies court cases and legislation about the rights of students who are exceptional is the:

   a. Due process clause of Public Law 94–142

   b. Right to Education Act of 1975

   c. Equal Protection Clause of the Fourteenth Amendment to the U.S. Constitution

   d. Individuals With Disabilities Education Act

2. Schools were first required to provide a free, appropriate public education to preschoolers with disabilities in:

   a. 1975

   b. 1986

   c. 1994

   d. 2000

3. Which of the following laws prohibits discrimination on the basis of disability in employment, services rendered by state and local governments, transportation, and telecommunication services?

   a. Individuals With Disabilities Education Act (IDEA)

   b. No Child Left Behind Act (NCLB)

  c. Education for All Handicapped Children Act (PL 94–142)

  d. Americans With Disabilities Act (ADA)

4. Which of the following is true about architectural accessibility—the removal of steps and other barriers that limit the participation of people with disabilities?

  a. Every building must be barrier free.

  b. Every method of transportation must be accessible to those who are disabled.

  c. Students with disabilities must have equal access to programs and services.

  d. A and B above

5. Which of the following is *not* required in Public Law 94–142, the Education for All Handicapped Children Act?

  a. Annual reporting on the performance and progress of all students, including students with disabilities

  b. Due process

  c. Education in a least restrictive environment (LRE)

  d. Individualized education program (IEP)

6. By law, decisions about eligibility for special education services must be made by:

  a. Principals

  b. School psychologists

  c. Multidisciplinary teams

  d. Parents

7. Under the Reading First legislation of the Bush administration, specialized reading services must be provided to:

a. Students in Grades 1 through 3 in Title 1 schools

b. Students with severe disabilities

c. All students, including students with disabilities and students with limited English proficiency

d. Students with reading disabilities

8. The protection in evaluation procedures provision of the law specifies all of the following except:

a. Tests must be administered in the language and form most likely to yield accurate information on what a child knows and can do academically, developmentally, and functionally unless not feasible to provide and administer.

b. Students must be assessed in their native language or mode of communication.

c. Parents must give their consent before a student can be tested.

d. Tests must be valid for the purposes for which they are used.

9. Which of the following was not decided in a U.S. Supreme Court case?

a. Segregation of schools is illegal because it denies equal protection and equal opportunity.

b. Children are "persons" under the Constitution and have civil rights independent of their parents.

c. Disruptive students with disabilities do not actually have to cause harm before removal from school; rather, they have to be judged substantially likely to cause harm.

d. Reimbursement for private school tuition is an appropriate form of relief for a court to grant.

10. Students with disabilities must be educated in a least restrictive environment. This means:

   a. They may not be placed in institutions.

   b. They have a right to be educated in general education classes.

   c. They have a right to be educated in the least restrictive setting in which they can be successful.

   d. Parents of students with disabilities cannot home-school the students.

11. A famous California court case, *Larry P. v. Riles,* addressed which of the following educational issues?

   a. Assessment of English language learners in their native language

   b. Bias in assessment of black students who were being considered for classes for mentally retarded students

   c. Exclusion of students with disabilities from public education

   d. Medical services for students with disabilities

REFLECTION

After you have responded to the multiple-choice self-assessment, provide brief answers to the following questions:

- Why did courts and legislatures get involved in the first place in matters of providing services to students with disabilities?
- How do the provisions of federal law increase the work of educational professionals?
- How would you know if a student was receiving an appropriate educational program?
- What changes in education of students with disabilities have resulted from federal legal cases and legislation?

Answer Key for Self-Assessments

1. c

2. b

3. d

4. c

5. a

6. c

7. a

8. b

9. c

10. c

11. b

On Your Own

☑ Obtain a copy of the Individuals With Disabilities Education Act (IDEA). Read it and make a list of things school personnel must do to comply with the law. Then look at the 2004 reauthorization of the 1997 IDEA and indicate changes in those requirements.

☑ Locate a summary of one of the U.S. Supreme Court cases discussed in this chapter. Write a report in which you list the plaintiffs, the defendants, and the nature of the complaint. Then describe the arguments made by each side and the Court's decision.

☑ Think about why it has taken so much legal activity to get school districts to allow students with disabilities to attend school and to provide appropriate services for those students.

Resources

BOOKS

Bateman, B., & Linden, M. A. (1998). *Better IEPs: How to develop legally correct and educationally useful programs* (3rd ed.). Longmont, CO: Sopris West Educational Services. An invaluable step-by-step guide to creating IEPs that are congruent with current law.

Cutler, B. (1993). *You, your child, and special education: A guide to making the system work.* Baltimore: Brookes. A practical guide to special education law and children's educational rights.

Rothstein, L. F. (1990). *Special education law.* White Plains, NY: Longman. Essential reading for those concerned about legal issues in special education. Rothstein's text is the most definitive treatment of special education law with a focus on how the law affects students with disabling conditions in the public school system. It reviews all the major judicial decisions, statutes, and regulations with interpretations, explanations of their meanings, and detailed discussions. It also will help teachers and administrators develop policies and make decisions that are consistent with legal requirements.

Telzrow, C. F., & Tankersley, M. (Eds.). (2000). *IDEA Amendments of 1997: Practice guidelines for school-based teams.* Bethesda, MD: National Association of School Psychologists. A comprehensive outline for many of the new implementations of

IDEA. All of the contributors are leaders in their respective fields who provide guidance through the practical implications for schools.

Wehman, P. (1993). *The ADA mandate for social change.* Baltimore: Brookes. This text provides a summary of the Americans With Disabilities Act and discusses its implications for individuals and organizations.

Journals and Articles

Individuals With Disabilities Education Law Reporter. This newsletter-type publication contains reviews of legislation and articles about the relevance of the law for students with disabilities. It includes summaries of the results of major national and state court cases. LRP Publications, 747 Dresher Rd., Box 980, Horsham, PA 19044–0980.

References

Amendments to the Education for All Handicapped Children Act, Pub. L. No. 99–457, 100 Stat. 1145 (1986).

Amendments to the Individuals With Disabilities Education Act, Pub. L. No. 105–17 (1997).

Americans With Disabilities Act, Pub. L. No. 101–336, 104 Stat. 327 (1990).

Beattie v. State Board of Education, 169 Wis. 231, 233, 172 N.W. 153, 154 (1919).

Brown v. Board of Education, 74 S. Ct. 686 (1954).

Burlington School Committee v. Massachusetts Department of Education, 471 U.S. 359, 105 S. Ct. 1996, 23 *Ed. Law Rptr.* 1189 (1985).

Cefalu v. East Baton Rouge Parish School Board, 25 IDELR 142 (5th Cir. 1996).

Civil Rights Act of 1964, Pub. L. No. 88–352, 78 Stat. 241 (1964).

Covarrubias v. San Diego Unified School District, Civ. No. 70–393–S (S.D. Cal., filed Feb. 1971; settled by consent decree, July 31, 1972).

Diana v. State Board of Education, C.A. No. C–70–37 R.F.P. (N.D. Cal. Filed Feb. 3, 1970).

Education for All Handicapped Children Act, Pub. L. No. 94–142, 89 Stat. 773 (1975).

Frederick L. v. Thomas, 419 F. Supp. 960 (E.D. Pa. 1976), aff'd 57 F. 2a373 (3rd Cir. 1977).

Goss v. Lopez, 419 U.S. 565 (1975).

Hairston v. Drosick, 423 F. Supp. 180 (S.D. W. Va. 1974).

Handicapped Children's Protection Act, Pub. L. No. 99–372, 100 Stat. 796 (1986).

Hendrick Hudson District Board of Education v. Rowley, 458 U.S. 176, 179–184 (1982).

Hobson v. Hansen, 269 F. Supp. 401 (D.C.D.C. 1967).

Honig v. Doe, 108 S. Ct. 592 (1988).

Individuals With Disabilities Education Act, Pub. L. No. 101–476, 104 Stat. 1141 (1990).

Individuals With Disabilities Education Improvement Act, Pub. L. No. 108–446 (2004).

Irving Independent School District v. Tatro, 468 U.S. 883 (1984).

Irving Independent School District v. Tatro, 104 S. Ct. 3371 (1984).

Kevin T. v. Elmhurst Community School District No. 205, 34 IDELR 202 (N.D. Ill. 2002).

Larry P. v. Riles, 343 F. Supp. 1306 (N.D. Cal. 1972), aff'd, 502 F. 2d 963 (9th Cir. 1974).

Lemon v. Bossier Parish School Board, 444 F. 2d 1440 (5th Cir. 1971).

Light v. Parkway School District, 21 IDELR 93 (8th Cir. 1994).

Lora v. New York City Board of Education, 456 F. Supp. 1211, 1275 (E.D.N.Y. 1978).

Mills v. Board of Education, 348 F. Supp. 866, 880 (D.D.C. 1972).

No Child Left Behind Act, Pub. L. No. 107–110, 115 Stat. 1425 (2001).

Panitch v. State of Wisconsin, 451 F. Supp. 132 (E.D. Wis. 1977).

PASE v. Hannon, 74C3586 (N.D. Ill. 1980).

Pennsylvania Association for Retarded Children v. Commonwealth of Pennsylvania, 334 F. Supp. 1257 (E.D. Pa. 1971); 343 F. Supp. 279 (E.D. Pa. 1972).

Rehabilitation Act, Pub. L. No. 93–112, 87 Stat. 357 (1973).

Smith v. Robinson, 104 S. Ct. 3457 (1984).

Timothy W. v. Rochester, New Hampshire, School District, 875 F. 2d 954 (1st Cir. 1989).

Tinker v. Des Moines Independent Community School District, 393 U.S. 503, 511 (1969).

U.S. Congress (1975). Education for All Handicapped Children Act of 1975, 20 U.S.C. §1401 et seq.

Washington v. Davis, 426 U.S. 229 (1976).

Watson v. City of Cambridge, 157 Mass. 561, 563, 32 N.E. 864, 864–65 (1893).

Wyatt v. Stickney, 325 F. Supp 781 (M.D. Ala. 1971), 334 F. Supp. 1341 (M.D. Ala. 1971), 344 F. Supp. 373 (M.D. Ala. 1972), sub nom Wyatt v. Aderholt, 503 F. 2d 1305 (5th Cir. 1974).

Yell, M. L. (1989). Honig v. Doe: The suspension and expulsion of handicapped students. *Exceptional Children, 56,* 60–69.

Zobrest v. Catalina Foothills School District, 113 S. Ct. 2462 (1993).

Index

Note: Numbers in **Bold** followed by a colon [:] denote the book number within which the page numbers are found.